CCSS **Genre** Realistic Fiction

W9-AKX-389

Essential Question
How do you express something that is important to you?

Every Picture Tells a Story

by Adrienne M. Frater

illustrated by Claire Mumford

Chapter 1
The Class Trip

"Before you leave today, I have two important announcements to make," says Ms. Frost. A ripple of excitement passes through the room, and Trudi's eyes sparkle as she waits expectantly to hear what her teacher has to say to the class.

"This Friday we're going on a field trip to visit a touring art exhibition, so please bring these permission slips back tomorrow." Most students smile as Ms. Frost passes out the slips, but some children frown. Not all of the class likes visiting art galleries.

Finished with handing out the slips, Ms. Frost continues, "The second announcement is that on the last Friday of this month, we'll be holding Grandparents' Day." This time it is Trudi's smile that switches to a frown.

Ms. Frost explains that those students who cannot bring grandparents can bring a parent or friend instead, but Trudi is still downcast. She only has one living grandparent, and Mormor, her grandmother, lives on a small island off the coast of Norway.

In each of the previous years, Trudi's next-door neighbor, Miss Silk, has been her substitute grandmother for Grandparents' Day. Trudi knows Miss Silk would be happy to come again, but this year, she wishes she could take Mormor by the hand and walk her through the classroom door. Trudi also knows that this is impossible.

That evening Trudi says to her parents, "I'm 11 years old, and I hardly know Mormor."

"There are plenty of photos," says Dad, "and you speak to her via the Internet."

"But she speaks so little English," Trudi replies, "and I speak so little Norwegian that I can't ask her the things I really want to know. She can't ask me things either."

Trudi lies in bed that night thinking. She does not expect Mormor to physically come to Grandparents' Day, but there must be another way she can introduce her to the class. If only she could figure out how.

On Friday Trudi sets off for school with her lunchbox and sketch pad. Along with the other students, she lines up in the school parking lot ready for the trip. The class is excited, and the noise on the bus sounds like a swarm of busy bees. Before long the bus pulls up in front of the art gallery.

"Bruegel—The People's Painter" reads the banner hanging above the gallery door. Ms. Frost has already explained that Bruegel painted four centuries ago, and although Trudi has been looking forward to seeing the exhibition, she hopes that his paintings will not be too dark and dreary.

The children line up and enter the gallery in pairs. They start at the beginning of the exhibition and walk their way through. Far from being dark and dreary, the paintings explode with life, and the closer Trudi looks, the more she sees happening in the pictures.

First they view Bruegel's paintings of the seasons. "These are called bird's-eye-view paintings," explains Ms. Frost. "At the time they were painted, few people could read and write, so Bruegel's paintings were a historical record of life in his time."

Ms. Frost smiles as she leads the children to a large painting on a wall at the far end of the gallery and says, "Now I want to show you my favorite." The painting is called *Children's Games*, and it shows a street filled with people in an old European town. The canvas is so jam-packed with detail that every time Trudi looks at it, she sees different things. Small groups of children are playing games, such as knucklebones, leapfrog, horsey, and blindman's buff. Some children are swinging on a post. Others are doing gymnastics, and a small boy has tied himself in a knot.

Trudi stares at the painting, captivated. Some of the children's games in the painting are similar to ones children play today, while others are completely different. Trudi looks at the long dresses the girls are wearing and thinks about how difficult it must have been to play in them.

Before long the other children begin to drift off to look at different paintings, but Trudi remains glued to the spot for the rest of the visit. She is amazed that so much information can be condensed into one painting. She is also intrigued by the idea that the painter has passed on all this meaningful information without using a single word.

Bruegel's painting gives Trudi an idea.

Chapter 3
Waiting for a Reply

The next day, Trudi rolls up her drawing, slips it into a tube, and mails it to Mormor. It takes about a week for mail to reach Norway, and Trudi hopes Mormor will call when it arrives.

At the same time, her class is preparing for Grandparents' Day, which is just ten days away. All the students are working on their projects, which are meant to compare their own hobbies with those of their grandparents (or grandparent substitutes). Trudi plans to have Mom ask Mormor about her hobbies when Mormor calls next. As time passes, however, and no call comes, Trudi starts working on her project and asks Mom her questions instead.

"What are Mormor's hobbies?" she asks. "How does she spend her time during the long Norwegian winter nights?"

"I'll show you," Mom says, taking her to the two framed tapestries hanging in the hall. One is of fishing boats unloading herring at a wharf. The other is of people skiing down a snow-covered mountainside through tall, green fir trees.

Trudi has lived with these tapestries all her life, but for the first time, she examines them closely. When she looks carefully at the skiers, she can see plumes of snow flying up behind them as they race down the slope.

"I never realized that Mormor made these," says Trudi, peering at all the tiny, intricate stitches. "They must have taken her a long time."

"Like many Norwegian women, your grandmother always has a tapestry in progress," Mom explains. "It's an art form in Norway, and when I look at these, I picture my mother sitting in front of the fire stitching."

When Mom says this, Trudi realizes how hard it must be for her mom to live apart from her own mother, and she gives her mom a hug.

At school the next day, Trudi finally finishes her project, and Ms. Frost displays it with the other students' work on a large table just inside the classroom door.

Then two days before Grandparents' Day, Dad asks Trudi, "Have you invited Miss Silk to Grandparents' Day yet?"

Trudi answers that she has not gotten around to it.

"Don't you think you should?" Dad asks.

Instead of going next door to invite Miss Silk, Trudi trudges to her room. She still has not heard from Mormor. She had hoped to introduce Mormor somehow on Grandparents' Day. Although she likes Miss Silk, Trudi has been imagining how wonderful it would be to introduce her real grandmother for so long that now she thinks, "I'd rather attend Grandparents' Day all by myself than go with someone who is not Mormor." Trudi is so agitated that she gets out a sheet of paper and starts to draw.

Whereas Trudi's first drawing was joyful, this one is an expression of sadness. It shows Trudi's school and the schoolyard with students hand in hand with their grandparents. They all look happy, but Trudi draws herself standing alone, looking mournful.

As Trudi puts down her pencil with a sigh, the doorbell rings. For a moment, she thinks it is the phone and is sure it will be Mormor calling. Then the doorbell rings a second time, and she calls out to her parents, "I'll get it."

It turns out to be a delivery man with a large parcel for her. She excitedly signs for the package and thanks the courier.

"What is it?" asks her mom, coming to the front door.

"I don't know," says Trudi, "but I do know it's very heavy and it comes from Norway!" Trudi's mom watches as she opens the package. Trudi looks with delight at the gift, realizing her problem is now solved.

Chapter 4
Grandparents' Day

Mormor calls later that night and asks Trudi's mom if the parcel has arrived.

"Yes," says Mom, "and Trudi's over the moon."

"What moon?"

"It's a saying we use in English." Trudi's mom switches to speaking Norwegian to explain the phrase. She tells Mormor that Trudi is absolutely thrilled and feels that she knows Mormor much better than before.

Mormor replies in Norwegian, "Please tell her the same. I am 'over the moon' about her drawing, too, and I now know my granddaughter better. It is such a coincidence that we were both working on similar but different projects at the same time."

The exchange takes time because of the translating, but when Mom is through, she passes the phone to Trudi. Mormor says "thank you" in Norwegian just as Trudi says the same thing in English, which makes them both laugh.

"Tell Mormor I'm taking her to Grandparents' Day," Trudi says to her mother.

On Grandparents' Day, Ms. Frost welcomes the grandparents, and one by one, the students introduce their guests. Trudi waits until everyone has been introduced, then raises her hand. "I'd like to introduce my grandmother now," she says, "but first I need an easel."

Once the easel is in place, Trudi places Mormor's gift on it and lets the audience have a long look. An excited, interested murmur that sounds like a bubbling stream runs through the room.

"My grandmother lives in Norway," Trudi begins. "I call her Mormor, which is Norwegian for 'mother's mother.' She can't be here in person, so she has sent this instead. For those of you who can't see the details, I'd like to explain what this tapestry tells me about my grandmother."

The audience listens intently as Trudi continues, "Here is her house. The pitch of the roof is steep so the snow can slide off. And here's her white cat, Snofnugg, which is Norwegian for 'snowflake.'"

One by one, Trudi points out the details in the tapestry, and by the time she is through, she is certain her classmates know Mormor almost as well as she does. They know the wild place where Mormor picks lingonberries to make jam. They know about the boathouses with their roofs of grass. They know the importance of the fishing boats tied up at the wharf. They can see the steep mountain peaks that Mormor looks at from her window. And they can see the huge arched bridge that joins Mormor's island to the mainland so that she does not have to cross by ferry anymore.

"Wait, I nearly forgot," says Trudi. "See this little Viking ship on the right? This tells me Mormor is as proud of her Scandinavian ancestry as I am."

When the guests have all left, Ms. Frost says, "Your grandmother's tapestry reminds me of Bruegel's paintings." Trudi is tempted to tell her teacher about the drawing she sent Mormor, but instead she just smiles and agrees.

"How did it go?" Mom asks when she picks Trudi up from school.

"I think everyone liked getting to know Mormor through her tapestry," says Trudi.

Back at home, Trudi hangs Mormor's tapestry on her bedroom wall. She stares at it for a while. Each time she looks, she discovers new things.

"That's a puffin," she thinks, examining the comical bird perched on a cliff face. "Exploring Mormor's tapestry is a little like opening a treasure chest."

As Trudi turns away from the tapestry, she spots her latest drawing sitting on her desk. She takes out her pencils and draws Mormor standing beside her, holding her hand. Next she erases her sad expression and replaces it with a cheerful smile.

"That's much better," she says, grinning.

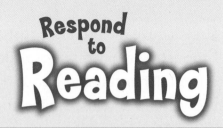

Summarize

Use important details from *Every Picture Tells a Story* to summarize the story. Your graphic organizer may help.

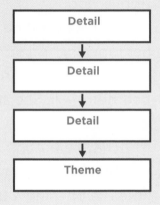

Text Evidence

1. How do you know that this story is realistic fiction?
   GENRE

2. Why did Trudi decide to draw a picture for her grandmother rather than write her a letter? How does her drawing a picture support the story's theme?
   THEME

3. What does the expression "a ripple of excitement" on page 2 mean? Why is it a metaphor?
   SIMILE AND METAPHOR

4. Write about the images Mormor chooses to include in the tapestry she sends to Trudi. How do these choices support the theme of the story?
   WRITE ABOUT READING

Compare Texts

Read a poem that expresses a bird's-eye view of Trudi's life in words.

THE EYES OF A BIRD

Pretend you're a bird aloft on the wind.

Fly with me over Trudi's small town.

With wings widespread, you hover ... glide ... soar ...

your keen eyes capturing what lies below.

Come, Mormor, come.

Streets slice the town into tree-lined squares

with houses painted white and green.

See the white wooden house

with a gray shingled roof.

In the yard is a plum tree,

in the plum tree a swing.

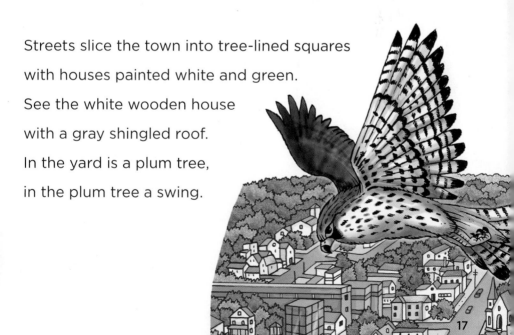

Swinging high, swinging low, Trudi thinks as she swings,

swings as she thinks—she's thinking of you.

Then she runs to the garden, picks peaches, digs carrots,

opens the hutch, and feeds her pet rabbit.

Come, Mormor, come.

Hot now, as hot as a red chili pepper—SPLASH!

Trudi dives into her friend's swimming pool.

Her arms cut the blue, her legs make foam.

Cooler now, she shivers as she dresses.

Come, Mormor, come.

Trudi runs down the street and into the library
brimming with books she loves to read.
Mystery, fantasy, fairy tale, adventure,
and books about Norway, for she reads about you.

For a moment, you lose her in a tangle of bushes.
There she is in her hideout, her own special place.
Let's leave her in peace, let's leave her to dream.
Spread your great wings and take to the sky.

Fly, Mormor, fly.

Make Connections

How does the speaker of the poem express what is
importance in Trudi's life? ESSENTIAL QUESTION

Compare the ways that the story and the poem
express similar ideas through a picture, a tapestry,
and a poem. Which way is most effective for you?
TEXT TO TEXT

Focus on
Literary Elements

Alliteration Alliteration is the repetition of the same beginning consonant sound in two or more words that are near each other. Poets often use alliteration to make the words or lines in a poem flow in a musical way.

Read and Find In *The Eyes of a Bird*, the poet uses alliteration several times. In the first two stanzas, "wings widespread" and "streets slice" are two examples of how the poet uses alliteration to connect words. Look for more instances of alliteration as you reread the poem.

Your Turn

Write a poem using alliteration. First, list five or six things from your daily life that you would like to share with a grandparent or another person in your life. Next, write a phrase or line that describes or expresses how you feel about each of these things, using alliteration. For example, "deliciously delightful dancing" or "perfect pet parrot." Read all the lines aloud and make changes if necessary to help your poem flow and sing. Share your poem with a friend. Have your words expressed things that are important to you?